1, 2, 3 [illegible] en

MW01706882

1, 2, 3 im Kindergarten

Susanne Böse Isabelle Dinter

Edition bi:libri

Heute ist ein großer Tag: Paul geht das erste Mal in den Kindergarten!
Mama packt seine Trinkflasche und die Brotzeitdose in den neuen Rucksack.
Was möchte Paul außerdem noch mitnehmen?

Today is a big day: Paul's going to kindergarten for the very first time!
Mommy puts his water bottle and lunch box in his new backpack.
What else does Paul want to take?

1

eins

one

Rucksack

backpack

Trinkflasche

water bottle

Teddy

teddy bear

Kennst du das Spiel, das Paul und Emre hier spielen?
Immer zwei Karten gehören zusammen. Wer die meisten Paare findet, hat gewonnen. Die Zwillinge Lena und Lisa schauen neugierig zu.

Do you know the game that Paul and Emre are playing?
There are always two cards that go together. Whoever finds the most pairs, wins. The twins Lena and Lisa are watching with curiosity.

Brille

glasses

Zwillinge

twins

Spielkarten

playing cards

2

zwei

two

Heute ist Gemüsetag. Es gibt Karottensuppe. Drei Kinder haben Küchendienst. Eins schneidet, eins kocht, eins deckt den Tisch. Hm, das wird lecker! Wenn Mama Paul um drei Uhr abholt, muss er ihr unbedingt davon erzählen.

Today is vegetable day. There's carrot soup for lunch. Three children have kitchen duty. One cuts the carrots, one cooks and one sets the table. Mmm, it's going to be yummy! When Mommy picks Paul up at three, he'll have to tell her about it.

3

drei

three

Karotten

carrots

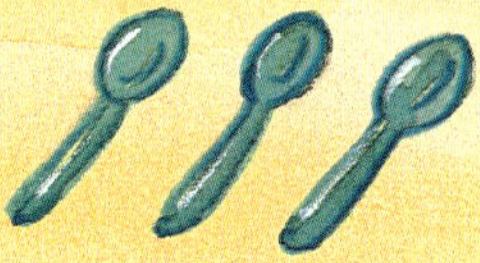

Löffel

spoons

Uhr

clock

Die Sonne scheint so schön! Deshalb geht es nach dem Essen hinaus in den Garten. Vier Kinder möchten rutschen. Und wie viele stehen auf der Brücke? Was machen Paul und Emre?

The sun is really shining! So everybody goes out to the playground after lunch. Four children want to go on the slide. And how many are standing on the bridge? What are Paul and Emre doing?

Marienkäfer

ladybug

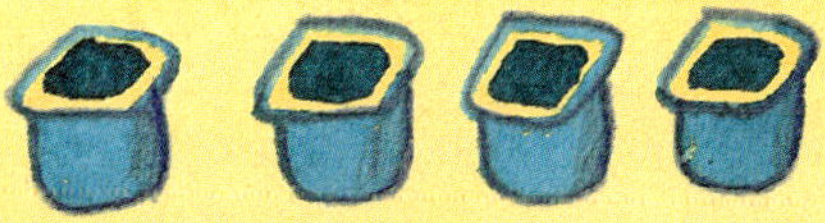

Förmchen

sand molds

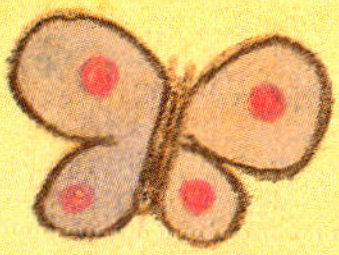

Schmetterling

butterfly

4

vier

four

Heute feiert Emre Geburtstag. Er bekommt eine tolle Krone. Wie alt wird er wohl? Erst singen die Kinder ein Lied. Dann schenken sie ihm fünf Murmeln. Darüber freut sich Emre sehr, denn er sammelt Murmeln.

Today is Emre's birthday. He gets a nice crown to wear. How old is he now? First the children sing a song. Then they give him his birthday present: five marbles. Emre is very happy, because he collects marbles.

fünf

five

Geburtstagskrone

birthday crown

Geburtstagskuchen

birthday cake

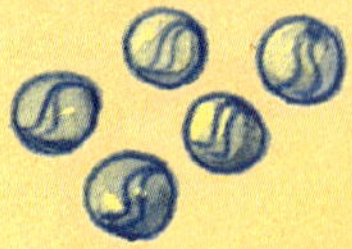

Murmeln

marbles

Turnen macht einen Riesenspaß! Emre bewundert Pauls neues Fußballtrikot. Welche Nummer hat er? Viele Kinder laufen auf der Bank. Kannst du sie zählen? Lisa schafft die meisten Purzelbäume: sechs Stück ohne Pause!

Tumbling is tons of fun! Emre admires Paul's new soccer jersey. Which number is he wearing? Lots of kids are walking on the bench. Can you count them? Lisa can do the most summersaults: six in a row!

Bälle

balls

Fußballtrikot

soccer jersey

Würfel

die / dice (pl.)

6

sechs

six

Die Woche hat sieben Tage. Paul kann sie aufsagen. Du auch?
Maria, die Erzieherin, liest den Kindern heute „Schneewittchen“ vor. Kennst du das Märchen? Dann weißt du bestimmt, wie viele Zwerge der Prinzessin helfen.

There are seven days in a week. Paul can name them all. Can you?
Maria, the teacher, is reading “Snow White” to the children today. Do you know that fairy tale? Then you surely know how many dwarfs help the princess.

sieben

seven

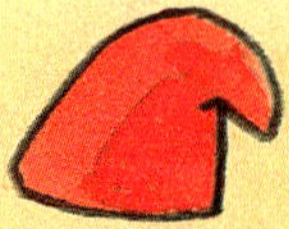

Zwergenmütze

dwarf hat

Spielzeugauto

toy car

Bauklötze

building blocks

Paul liebt es, wenn die Kinder in den Wald gehen. Da gibt es viel zu entdecken. Schau, da krabbelt eine Spinne! Weißt du, wie viele Beine sie hat? Paul sucht gerne Kastanien. Die sind so wunderbar glatt.

Paul loves it when they go into the woods. There's a lot to discover. Look, there's a spider crawling over there! Do you know how many legs it has? Paul likes to look for chestnuts. They feel so wonderfully smooth.

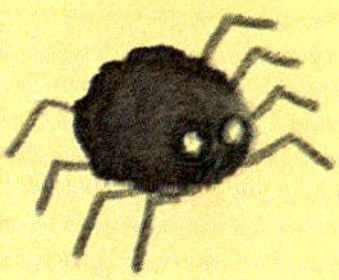

Spinne
spider

Tannenzapfen
pine cones

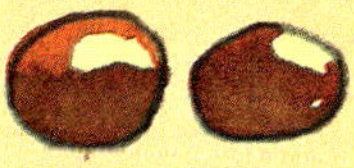

Kastanien
chestnuts

8

acht
eight

Was für ein kunterbuntes Bild Paul da malt! Wie viele Farben benutzt er? Kennst du sie schon? Lena ist Lehrerin in der Kuscheltierschule. Wie viele Schüler hat sie? Und welche Zahl lernen sie heute wohl kennen?

What a bright picture Paul is coloring! How many colors is he using? Do you know all of them? Lena is playing teacher in the stuffed animal school. How many students does she have? And which number are they learning today?

neun	Kuscheltier	Tafel	Buntstifte
nine	stuffed animal	blackboard	colored pencils

Paul und Emre kitzeln sich an den nackten Füßen. Wie viele Zehen hast du? Und wie viele Finger? Kaisha trägt eine Perlenkette mit zehn Perlen. Und Maria? Die hat zehn lustige Sommersprossen!

Paul and Emre are tickling each other's bare feet. How many toes do you have? And how many fingers? Kaisha is wearing a beaded necklace with ten beads. And Maria? She has 10 jolly freckles!

		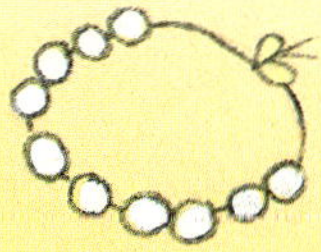	10
Finger	Sommersprossen	Perlenkette	zehn
fingers	freckles	beaded necklace	ten

Nachts hat Paul einen lustigen Traum.
Pass genau auf: Alles ist durcheinander.
Nur eine Sache stimmt. Ahnst du, welche?

That night Paul has a silly dream.
Look closely: everything is mixed up.
Just one thing is right. Can you tell which?

1	2	3	4	5
eins	zwei	drei	vier	fünf
one	two	three	four	five

6	7	8	9	10
sechs	sieben	acht	neun	zehn
six	seven	eight	nine	ten

Hurra, jetzt herrscht wieder Ordnung. Du kannst alle Zahlen noch einmal entdecken. Was gibt es nur einmal? Wo stecken die 5 und die 6? Und wovon gibt es zehn?

Hooray, now everything's back to normal. You can find all of the right numbers again. What is there only one of? Where are the numbers 5 and 6? And what are there ten of?

Lösungen:

Habt Ihr alle Fehler in Pauls Traum gefunden?

1: Es gibt nur eine Kirsche statt zwei.
2: Die Zahl auf Pauls Trikot ist die 2 sollte aber die 6 sein.
3: Die Zwillinge, Lisa und Lena, sind in Pauls Traum Drillinge.
4: Emre hat vier Augen statt zwei.
5: Marias zehn Sommersprossen gibt es hier nur fünfmal.
6: Paul hält eine Spinne in der Hand und hat sechs Finger!
7: Maria trägt Emres Geburtstagskrone mit der Nummer 7. Er ist aber erst fünfgeworden.
8: Emre trägt Kaishas Perlenkette und es fehlen zwei Perlen.
9: Lenas Tafel hat die Zahl 9 drauf. Das stimmt!
10: Die Spinne in Pauls Hand hat zehn Beine, dabei hat eine Spinne immer acht Beine.

Did you find all of the mistakes in Paul's dream?

1: There is only one cherry, instead of two.
2: The number 2 is on Paul's soccer jersey, but it should be the 6.
3: The twins, Lena and Lisa, are triplets in Paul's dream.
4: Emre has four eyes instead of two.
5: Maria's ten freckles are now only five.
6: Paul is holding a spider in his hand and has six fingers!
7: Maria is wearing Emre's birthday crown with the number 7 on it. But he just turned five.
8: Emre's wearing Kaisha's beaded necklace, and there are two beads missing.
9: Lena's blackboard has the number 9 on it. That's right!
10: The spider in Paul's hand has ten legs, but spiders always have eight legs.